Thennif

Photo by William Gibson/Martha Swope Associates
A scene from the New York Shakespeare Festival production of "Fires in the Mirror: Crown Heights, Brooklyn and Other Identities." Set design by James Youmans.

FIRES IN THE MIRROR:

Crown Heights, Brooklyn and Other Identities

BY ANNA DEAVERE SMITH

★

DRAMATISTS
PLAY SERVICE
INC.

FIRES IN THE MIRROR: Crown Heights, Brooklyn and Other Identities
Copyright © 1993, 1997, Anna Deavere Smith

All Rights Reserved

This play is dedicated
to the memory of my father,
Deaver Young Smith, Jr.
and of my stage manager,
Mr. Richard Hollabaugh

FIRES IN THE MIRROR: CROWN HEIGHTS, BROOKLYN AND OTHER IDENTITES is part of a series developed by Anna Deavere Smith called ON THE ROAD: A SEARCH FOR AMERICAN CHARACTER. The Crown Heights material in FIRES IN THE MIRROR was created for and performed as part of George C. Wolfe's Festival of New Voices at the New York Shakespeare Festival (Joanne Akalaitis, Artistic Director), in New York City, in December, 1991. It was directed by Christopher Ashley; the scene design was by James Youmans; the costume design was by Candice Donnelly; the lighting design was by Debra J. Kletter; the music was composed by Joseph Jarman and the production stage manager was Karen Moore. The show was performed by Anna Deavere Smith.

TABLE OF CONTENTS

CHARACTERS

NTOZAKE SHANGE — Playwright, poet, novelist

ANONYMOUS LUBAVITCHER WOMAN — Preschool teacher

GEORGE C. WOLFE — Playwright, director, producing director of the New York Shakespeare Festival

AARON M. BERNSTEIN — Physicist at Massachusetts Institute of Technology.

ANONYMOUS GIRL — Junior high school black girl of Haitian descent. Lives in Brooklyn near Crown Heights.

THE REVEREND AL SHARPTON — Well-known New York activist, minister.

RIVKAH SIEGAL — Lubavitcher woman, graphic designer.

ANGELA DAVIS — Author, orator, activist, scholar. Professor in the History of Consciousness Department at the University of California, Santa Cruz.

MONIQUE "BIG MO" MATTHEWS — Los Angeles rapper.

LEONARD JEFFRIES — Professor of African-American Studies at City University of New York, former head of the department.

LETTY COTTIN POGREBIN — Author *Deborah, Golda, and Me, Being Female and Jewish in America.* One of the founding editors of *Ms.* magazine.

MINISTER CONRAD MOHAMMED — New York minister for the Honorable Louis Farrakhan.

ROBERT SHERMAN — Director, Mayor of the City of New York's Increase the Peace Corps.

RABBI JOSEPH SPIELMAN — Spokesperson in the Lubavitch community.

THE REVEREND CANON DOCTOR HERON SAM — Pastor, St. Mark's, Crown Heights Church.

ANONYMOUS YOUNG MAN #1 — Crown Heights resident.

MICHAEL S. MILLER — Executive Director at the Jewish Community Relations Council.

HENRY RICE — Crown Heights resident.

NORMAN ROSENBAUM — Brother of Yankel Rosenbaum. A barrister from Australia.

ANONYMOUS YOUNG MAN #2 — African-American young man, late teens, early twenties. Resident of Crown Heights.

SONNY CARSON — Activist.

RABBI SHEA HECHT — Lubavitcher rabbi, spokesperson.

RICHARD GREEN — Director, Crown Heights Youth Collective. Co-director Project CURE, a Black-Hasidic basketball team that developed after the riots.

ROSLYN MALAMUD — Lubavitcher resident of Crown Heights.

REUVEN OSTROV — Lubavitcher youth, member, project CURE; at the time of the riot, was seventeen years old. Worked as assistant chaplain at Kings County Hospital.

CARMEL CATO — Father of Gavin Cato. Crown Heights resident, originally from Guyana.

IDENTITY

NTOZAKE SHANGE

The Desert

This interview was done on the phone at about 4:00 P.M. Philadelphia time. The only cue Ntozake gave about her physical appearance was that she took one earring off to talk on the phone. On stage we placed her upstage center in an arm chair, smoking. Then we placed her standing, downstage.

Hummmm.
Identity —
it, is, uh … in a way it's, um … it's sort of, it's uh …
it's a psychic sense of place
it's a way of knowing I'm not a rock or that tree?
I'm this other living creature over here?
And it's a way of knowing that no matter where I put myself
that I am not necessarily
what's around me.
I am part of my surroundings
and I become separate from them
and it's being able to make these differentiations clearly
that lets us have an identity
and what's inside our identity
is everything that's ever happened to us.
Everything that's ever happened
to us as well as our responses to it
'cause we might be alone in a trance state,
someplace like the desert
and we begin to feel as though
we are part of the desert —
if we are part of the desert
which we are right at that minute —
but we are not the desert,

uh ...

we are part of the desert,

and when we go home

we take with us that part of the desert that the desert
gave us,

but we're still not the desert.

It's an important differentiation to make because you
don't know

what you're giving if you don't know what you have and
you don't

know what your taking if you don't know what's yours
and what's

somebody else's.

ANONYMOUS LUBAVITCHER WOMAN

Static

This interview was actually done on the phone. Based on what she told me she was doing, and on the three visits I made to her home for other interviews, I devised this physical scene. A Lubavitcher woman, in a wig, and loose-fitting clothes. She is in her mid-thirties. She is folding clothes. There are several children around. Three boys of different ages are lying together on the couch. The oldest is reading to the younger two. A teen-age girl with long hair, a button-down-collar shirt, and skirt is sweeping the floor.

Well,
it was um,
getting towards the end of Shabbas,
like around five in the afternoon,
and it was summertime
and sunset isn't until about eight, nine o'clock,
so there were still quite a few hours left to go
and my baby had been playing with the knobs on the
    stereo system
then all of a sudden he pushed the button —
the *on* button —
and all of a sudden came blaring out,
at full volume,
sort of like a half station
of polka music.
But just like with the static,
it was blaring, blaring
and we can't turn off,
we can't turn off electrical,
you know electricity, on Shabbas.
So um,

uh ...
there was —
we just were trying to ignore it,
but a young boy that was visiting us,
he was going nuts already, he said
it was giving him such a headache could we do something
    about it,
couldn't we get a baby
to turn it off;
we can't make the baby turn it off but if the baby,
but if a child under three
turns something on or turns something off it's not
    considered against the Torah,
so we put the baby by it and tried to get the baby to turn
    it off,
he just probably made it worst,
so the guest was so uncomfortable that I said I would go
    outside
and see if I can find someone who's not Jewish and see if
    they would
like to —
see if they could turn it off,
so you can have somebody who's not Jewish can do a simple
    act like
turning on the light or turning off the light,
and I hope I have the law correct,
but you can't ask them to do it directly.
If they wanna do it of their own free will —
and hopefully they would get some benefit from it too,
so I went outside
and I saw
a little
boy in the neighborhood
who I didn't know and didn't know me —
not Jewish, he was black and he wasn't wearing a
    yarmulke because you can't —
so I went up to him and I said to him
that my radio is on really loud and I can't turn it off,

could he help me
so he looked at me a little crazy like,
Well?
And I said I don't know what to do,
so he said okay,
so he followed me into the house
and he hears this music on so loud
and so unpleasant
and so
he goes over to the
stereo
and he says, "You see this little button here
that says on and off?
Push that in
and that turns if off."
And I just sort of stood there looking kind of dumb
and then he went and pushed it,
and we laughed that he probably thought:
And people say Jewish people are really smart and they
don't know
how to turn off the their radios.

GEORGE C. WOLFE

101 Dalmations

The Mondrian Hotel in Los Angeles. Morning, Sunny. A very nice room. George is wearing denim jeans, a light blue denim shirt, and white leather tennis shoes. His hair is in a pony tail. He wears tortoise/wire spectacles. He is drinking tea with milk. The tea is served on a tray, the cups and the tea pot are delicate porcelain. George is sitting on a sofa, with his feet up on the coffee table.

I mean I grew up on a black —
a one-block street —
that was black.
My grandmother lived on that street
My cousins lived around the corner.
I went to this
Black — Black —
private Black grade school
where
I was extraordinary.
Everybody there was extraordinary.
You were told you were extraordinary.
It was very clear
that I could not go to see *101 Dalmations* at the Capital
    Theatre
because it was segregated.
And at the same time
I was treated like I was the most extraordinary creature
    that had
been born.
So I'm on my street in my house,
at my school —
and I was very spoiled too —
so I was treated like I was this special special creature.

And then I would go beyond a certain point
I was treated like I was insignificant.
Nobody was
hosing me down or calling me nigger.
It was just that I was insignificant.
(Slight pause.)
You know what I mean so it was very clear of
(Teacup of saucer strike twice on "very clear.")
where my extraordinariness lived.
You know what I mean.
That I was extraordinary as long as I was Black.
(Laugh.)
But I am — not — going — to place myself
(Pause.)
in relationship to your whiteness.
I will talk about your whiteness if we want to talk about
    that.
But I,
but what,
that which,
what I —
what am I saying?
My blackness does not resis — ex — re —
exist in relationship to your whiteness.
(Pause.)
You know
(Not really a question, more like a hum. Slight pause.)
it does not exist in relationship to —
it *exists*
it exists.
I come —
you know what I mean —
Like I said, I, I, I,
I come from —
it's a very com*plex*,
it's con*fused*,
neu-rotic,
at times destructive

reality, but it is completely
and totally a reality
contained and, and,
and full unto itself.
It's complex.
It's demonic.
It's ridiculous.
It's absurd.
It's evolved.
It's all the stuff.
That's the way I grew up.
(Slight pause.)
So that *therefore* —
and then you're White —
(Quick beat.)
And then there's a point when,
and then these two things come into contact.

MIRRORS

AARON M. BERNSTEIN

Mirrors and Distortions

Evening, Cambridge, Massachusetts. Fall. He is a man in his fifties, wearing a sweater and a shirt with a pen guard. He is seated at a round wooden table with a low-hanging lamp.

Okay, so a mirror is something that reflects light.
It's the simplest instrument to understand,
okay?
So a simple mirror is just a flat
reflecting
substance, like,
for example,
it's a piece of glass which is silvered on the back,
okay?
Now the notion of distortion also goes back into literature,
okay?
I'm trying to remember from art —
You probably know better than I.
You know you have a pretty young woman and she looks in
    a mirror
and she's a witch
(He laughs.)
because she's evil on the inside.
That's not a real mirror,
as everyone knows —
where
you see the inner thing.
Now that really goes back in literature.
So everyone understood that mirrors don't distort,
so that was a play
not on words
but a concept.

But physicists do
talk about distortion.
It's a big
subject, distortions.
I'll give you an example —
if you wanna see the
stars
you make a big
reflecting mirror —
that's one of the ways —
you make a big telescope
so you can gather in a lot of light
and then it focuses at a point
and then there's always something called the circle of
    confusion.
So if ya don't make the thing perfectly spherical or
    perfectly
parabolic
then,
then, uh, if there are errors in the construction
which you can see, it's easy, if it's huge,
then you're gonna have a circle of confusion,
you see?
So that's the reason for making the
telescope as large as you can,
because you want that circle
to seem smaller,
and you want to easily see errors in the construction.
So, you see, in physics it's very practical —
if you wanna look up in the heavens
and see the stars as well as you can
without distortion.
If you're counting stars, for example,
and two look like one,
you've blown it.

HAIR

ANONYMOUS GIRL

Look in the Mirror

Morning. Spring. A teen-age Black girl of Haitian descent. She has hair which is straightened, and is wearing a navy blue jumper and a white shirt. She is seated in a stairwell at her junior high school in Brooklyn.

When I look in the mirror ...
I don't know.
How did I find out I was Black ...
(Tongue sound.)
When I grew up and I look in the mirror and saw I was
    Black.
When I look at my parents,
That's how I knew I was Black.
Look at my skin.
You Black?
Black is beautiful.
I don't know.
That's what I always say.
I think White is beautiful too.
But I think Black is beautiful too.
In my class nobody is White, everybody's Black,
and some of them is Hispanic.
In my class
you can't call any of them Puerto Ricans.
They despise Puerto Ricans, I don't know why.
They think that Puerto Ricans are stuck up and everything.
They say, Oh my Gosh my nail broke, look at that cute guy
    and everything.
But they act like that themselves.
They act just like White girls.
Black girls is not like that.
Please, you should be in my class.

Like they say that Puerto Ricans act like that
and they don't see that they act like that themselves.
Black girls, they do bite off the Spanish girls,
they bite off of your clothes.
You don't know what that means? Biting off?
Like biting off somebody's clothes.
Like cop, following?
and last year they used to have a lot of girls like that.
They come to school with a style, right?
And if they see another girl with that style?
"Oh my gosh look at her."
"What she think she is?"
"She tryin' to bite off of me in some way!"
"No don't be bitin' off of my sneakers!"
or like that.
Or doin' a hairstyle.
I mean Black people are into hairstyles.
So they come to school, see somebody with a certain style,
they say "uh-huh I'm gonna get me one just like that uh-huh,"
that's the way Black people are
Yea-ah!
They don't like people doing that to them
and they do that to other people!
So the Black girls will follow the Spanish girls!
The Spanish girls don't bite off of us.
Some of the Black girls follow them.
But they don't mind.
They don't care.
They follow each other.
Like there's three girls in my class,
they from the Dominican Republic.
They all stick together like glue.
They all three best friends.
They don't follow nobody,
like there's none of them lead or anything.
They don't hang around us either.
They're
by themselves.

THE REVEREND AL SHARPTON

Me and James's Thing

Early afternoon. Fall. A small room that is a part of a suite of offices in a building on West Fifty-seventh Street and Seventh Avenue in New York. A very large Black man with straightened hair. Reverend Sharpton's hair is in the style of James Brown's hair. He is wearing a suit, colorful tie, and a gold medallion that was given to him by Martin Luther King, Jr. Reverend Sharpton has a pinky ring, and a very resonant voice even in this small room. There is a very built, very tall man who sits behind me during the interview. Reverend Sharpton's face is much younger, and more innocent than it appears to be in the media. His humor is in his face. He is very direct. The interview only lasts fifteen minutes because he had been called out of a meeting in progress to do the interview.

James Brown raised me.
Uh ...
I never had a father.
My father left when I was ten.
James Brown took me to the beauty parlor one day
and made my hair like his.
And made me promise
to wear it like that
'til I die.
It's a personal family thing
between me and James Brown.
I always wanted a father
and he filled that void.
And the strength that he's demonstrated —
I don't know anybody that reached his heights,

and then had to go as low as he did and come back.
And I think if anybody I met in life deserved that type of
tribute from
somebody
that he wanted a kid
to look like him
and be like his son ...
I just came home from spending a weekend with him now
uh, uh,
I think James deserved that.
And just like
he was the father I never had,
his kids never even visited him when he was in jail.
So I was like the kid he never had.
And if I had to choose between arguing with people
    about my
hairstyle
or giving him that one tribute
he axed,
I'd rather give him that tribute
because he filled a void for me.
And I really don't give a damn
who doesn't understand it.
Oh, I know not you, not you.
The press and everybody do
their thing on that.
It's a personal thing between me and James Brown.
And just like
in other communities
people do their cultural thing
with who they wanna look like,
uh,
there's nothing wrong with me doing
that with James.
It's, it's, *us.*
I mean in the fifties it was a slick.
It was acting like White folks.

But today
people don't wear their hair like that.
So it's certainlih not
a reaction to Whites
It's me and James's thing.

RIVKAH SIEGAL

Wigs

*Early afternoon, Spring. The kitchen of an apartment in
Crown Heights. A very pretty Lubavitcher woman, with clear
eyes and a direct gaze, wearing a wig and a knit sweater,
that looks as though it might be hand knit. A round wooden
table. Coffee mug. Sounds of children playing in the street
are outside. A neighbor, a Lubavitcher woman with light
blond hair who no longer wears the wig, observes the interview at the table.*

Your hair —
It only has to be —
there's different,
uhm,
customs in different
Hasidic groups.
Lubavitch
the system is
it should be two inches
long.
It's —
some groups
have
the custom
to shave their
heads.
There's —
the reason is
when you go to the mikva [bath]
you may, maybe
it's better if it's short
because of what you —

the preparation
that's involved
and that
you have to go under the water.
The hair has a tendency to float
and you have to be completely submerged
including your hair.
So ...
And I got married
when I was a little older,
and I really wanted to be married
and I really wanted to, um ...
In some ways I was eager to cover my head.
Now if I had grown up in a Lubovitch household
and then had to cut it,
I don't know what that would be like.
I really don't.
But now that I'm wearing the wig,
you see,
with my hair I can keep it very simple
and I can change it all the time
So with a wig you have to have like five wigs if you want to
     do that
But I, uh
I feel somehow like it's fake,
I feel like it's not me.
I try to be as much myself as I can,
and it just
bothers me
that I'm kind of fooling the world.
I used to go to work.
People ...
and I would wear a different wig,
and they'd say I like your new haircut
and I'd say it's not mine!
You know,
and it was very hard for me to say it

and
it became very difficult.
I mean, I've gone through a lot with wearing wigs and
   not wearing
wigs.
It's been a big issue for me.

RACE

ANGELA DAVIS

Rope

Morning. Spring. Oakland, California. In reality this inter-
view was done on the phone, with myself and Thulani
Davis. Thulani and I were calling from an office at the
Public Theatre. We do not know exactly what she was doing
or wearing.

Race um —
of course
for many years in the history
of African Americans in this country —
was synonymous with the community.
As a matter of fact
we were race women and race men.
Billie Holiday for example,
called herself a race woman,
because she supported the community
and as a child growing up in the South
my assumptions were
that if anybody in the race
came under attack
then I had to be there
to support that person,
to support the race.
I was saying to my students just the other day,
I said,
if in 1970
when I was
in jail,

someone had told me
that in 1991,
a Black man,
who
said that his, um ...
hero —
(Increased volume, speed, and energy.)
one of his heroes
was Malcolm X —
would be nominated to the Supreme Court
I would have celebrated
and I don't think it would have been possible at that
    time
to convince me
that I would
be absolutely opposed,
to a Black candidate —
I mean like absolutely —
(A new attack, more energy.)
or that if anyone would have told me that
a *woman* ...
would finally be elected to the Supreme Court,
it would have been very difficult,
as critical as I am with respect to feminism,
as critical as I have always been with what I used to call,
you know, narrow nationalism?
I don't think
it would have been possible to convince me, that things
    would have so absolutely
shifted that
someone could have evoked
the specter of lynching
on national television
and that specter of lynching would be used to violate
    our history.
And I still feel that

we have to point out the racism involved
in the razing of a Black man
and a Black woman
in that way.
I mean [Ted] Kennedy was sitting right there
and it had never occurred to anyone to bring
     him up
before
the world,
which is not to say that I don't think it should
     happen.
And it is actually a sign of how we,
in our various oppressed
marginalized communities,
have been able to turn
terrible acts of racism directed against us
into victory ...
And therefore I think
Anita Hill did that,
and so it's very complicated,
but I have no problems aligning myself politically
against Clarence Thomas in a real passionate way,
but at the same time I can talk about the racism
     that led
to the possibility
of constructing these kinds of hearings
and
the same thing with Mike Tyson.
So I guess that would be,
um ...
the way in which I would begin to look at
     community,
and would therefore think
that race has become, uh,
an increasingly obsolete way

of constructing community
because it is based on unchangeable
immutable biological
facts
in a very pseudo-scientific way,
alright?
Now
racism is entirely different
because see *racism*,
uh,
actually I think
is
at the origins of this concept of race.
It's not —
it's not the other way around,
that there were racists,
and then the racists —
one race came to dominate
the others.
As a matter of fact
in order for European colonialists
to attempt
to conquer the world,
to colonize the world,
they had to construct this notion
of,
uh,
the populations of the earth being divided into
    certain,
uh,
firm biological, uh,
communities,
and that's what I think we have to go back and
    look at.
So when I use the word race now I put it in
    quotations.

Because if we don't transform
this ... this intransigent
rigid
notion of race,
we will be caught up in this cycle
of genocidal
violence
that, um,
is at the origins of our history.
So I think —
and I'm
I'm convinced —
and this is what I'm working on in my political
    practice right now —
is that we have to find ways of coming together in a
    different way,
not the old notion of coalition in which we anchor
    ourselves very solidly
in our,
um,
communities,
and simply voice
our
solidarity with other people.
I'm not suggesting that we do not anchor ourselves
    in our communities;
I feel very anchored in,
um,
my various communities,
but I think that,
you know,
to use a metaphor, the rope
attached to that anchor should be long enough to
    allow us to move
into other communities
to understand and learn.

I've been thinking a lot about the need to make more
    intimate
these connections and associations and to really take on
    the responsibility
of learning.
What I'm interested in is communities
that are not static,
that
can change, that can respond to new historical needs.
So I think it's a very exciting moment.

RHYTHM

MONIQUE "BIG MO" MATTHEWS

Rhythm and Poetry

In reality this interview was done on an afternoon in the spring of 1989, while I was in residence at the University of California, Los Angeles, as a fellow at the Center for Afro-American Studies. Mo was a student of mine. We were sitting in my office, which was a narrow office, with sunlight. I performed Mo in many shows, and in the course of performing her, I changed the setting to a performance setting, with microphone. I was inspired by a performance that I saw of Queen Latifah in San Francisco, and by Mo's behavior in my class, which was performance behavior, to change the setting to one that was more theatrical, since Mo's everyday speech was as theatrical as Latifah's performance speech. Speaking directly to the audience, pacing the stage.

And she say, "This is for the fellas,"
and she took off all her clothes and she had on a leotard
that had all cuts and stuff in it,
and she started doin' it on the floor.
They were like
"Go girl!"
People like, "That look really stink."
But that's what a lot of female rappers do —
like to try to get off,
they sell they body or pimp they body
to, um, get play.
And you have people like Latifah who doesn't, you know,
she talks intelligent.
You have Lyte who's just hard and people are scared by her hardness,
her strength of her words.
She encompasses that whole, New York-street sound.

It's like, you know, she'll like ...
what's a line?
What's a line
like "Paper Thin,"
"IN ONE EAR AND RIGHT OUT THE OTHUH"
It's like,
"I don't care what you have to say,
I'm gittin' done what's gotta be done.
Man can't come across me.
A female she can't stand against me.
I'm just the toughest, I'm just the hardest/You just can't
      come up
against me/if you do you gonna get waxed!"
It's like a lot of my songs,
I don't know if I'm gonna get blacklisted for it.
The image that I want is a strong strong African strong
      Black woman
and I'm not down with what's going on, like big Daddy
      Kane had a song
out called "Pimpin' Ain't Easy," and he sat there and he
      talk for the
whole song, and I sit there I wanna slap him, I wanna slap
      him so
hard, and he talks about, it's one point he goes, yeah
um,
"Puerto Rican girls, Puerto Rican girls call me Papi and
White girls,
even White girls say I'm a hunk!"
I'm like,
"What you mean 'even'?
Oh! Black girls ain't good enough for you huh?"
And one of my songs has a line that's like
"PIMPIN' AIN'T EASY BUT WHORIN' AIN'T PROPER.
      RESPECT AND
CHERISH THE ORIGINAL MOTHER."
And a couple of my friends were like,
"Aww, Mo, you good but I can't listen to you 'cause you be
      Men

bashin'."
I say,
"It ain't men bashin', it's female assertin'."
Shit.
I'm tired of it.
I'm tired of my friends just acceptin'
that they just considered to be a ho.
You got a song,
"Everybody's a Hotty."
A "hotty" means you a freak, you a ho,
and it's like Too Short
gets up there and he goes,
"B I AYYYYYYYYYYYE."
Like he stretches "bitch" out for as long as possible,
like you just a ho and you can't be saved,
and 2 Live Crew.... "We want some pussy," and the girls!
    "La le la le la le la,"
it's like my friends say,
"Mo, if you so bad how come you don't never say nothin'
    about 2
Live Crew?"
When I talk about rap,
and I talk about people demeaning rap,
I don't even mention them
because they don't understand the fundamentals of rap.
Rap, rap
is basically
broken down
Rhythm
and Poetry.
And Poetry is expression.
Poetry is like
intelligence.
You just release it all and if you don't have a complex
    rhyme
it's like,
"I'm goin' to the store."
What rhymes with store?

More, store, for, more, bore
"I'm going to the store I hope I don't get bored,"
it's like,
WHAT YOU SAYIN', MAN? WHO CARES?"
You have to have something that flows.
You have to be def,
D–E–F.
I guess I have to think of something for you that ain't
    slang.
Def is dope, dope is live
when you say somethin's dope
it means it is the epitome of the experience
and you have to be def by your very presence
because you have to make people happy.
And we are living in a society where people are not happy
    with their everyday lives.

SEVEN VERSES

LEONARD JEFFRIES

Roots

3:00 P.M. Wednesday, November 20, 1991. A very large conference room in the African-American Studies Department at CUNY. Drawn venetian blinds, fluorescent lighting. Dr. Jeffries wears a light, multicolored African top, and a multicolored African hat. His shoes are black functional shoes, like the shoes to a uniform. He sits facing the table, and often sits back with the chair back from the table, often touches the table, and often sits back with the chair on its back legs only. Sometimes he scratches his head by throwing his hat forward on his head with great ease and authority. There is a bodyguard, a large heavy-set African-American man, present.

People are asking who is this guy Jeffries?
When they find out my background they're gonna be
surprised.
They are gonna find out that I was even related to Alex
Haley.
In fact I was a major consultant for *Roots.*
In fact there might not have been a *Roots* without me.
Now when I say that,
that's my own personal in-group joke wit' Alex.
He was in Philadelphia
getting his ticket to go down to Jamaica
and
Roots was lost.
He had it in a duffle bag,
a big duffle bag like this,
the whole manuscript.
It was lost in the airport of Philadelphia.
I got on my horse and ran around the airport of
Philadelphia

and found *Roots.*
So that's my joke.
He had this manuscript,
Alex didn't have anything else but this manuscript.
Now if he had lost that, that would have been it.
He didn't have any photocopies.
Alex did everything on a shoestring.
uhm
so for him to deny me now ...
He never even acknowledged
Pat
Alexander
his girlfriend/secretary who he had paid with affection and
    not with
resources.
So I didn't expect him to acknowledge me.
He called me to come down.
I called my wife who was working on her Ph.D. at Yale.
I said, "Rosalind, Alex wants us to come down to
    Brunswick, Georgia,
they're filming *Roots.*"
She said yes she'd come down and we'd go, then she called
    me back.
She said, "I got too much work," so I went down to
    Brunswick, Georgia.
He introduced me to Margulies,
who was the, um, director
of *Roots,*
as the leading expert in American on Africa, and I said,
    "Wow," to
myself "that's kind of high."
When Margulies said,
"That makes me number two," then I realized what Alex was
    doing to keep *Roots* honest.
So for two weeks I tried to change *Roots.*
Alex would say, "Wait a
minute, let's consult the experts."
After two weeks they got tired of me, sat me down

and said, "Dr. Jeffries," at lunch,
"we are very happy to have you here
but we just bought the rights to the book *Roots*
and we are under no obligation to maintain the integrity of
the book
and we certainly don't have to deal with the truth of Black
history."
Now,
this was a wipeout for me
I
I, there's been very few traumatic
moments
(Longest pause in his text.)
uh, just to think.
Now I wasn't even prepared for this
but Pat had called me before and said,
"Len, I'm looking at this document and I don't know what
to make of it."
I said, "What is it Pat. What is it?"
And I knew she was nervous, she said,
"I'm reading a contract that says
"*Roots* has been sold to David Wolper and their heirs
forever 'n ever.
(He is thumping his hand on table.)
and their heirs forever 'n ever."
Alex had signed the contract for fifty-thousand dollars.
(He is thumping his hand on table.)
Fifty thousand dollars for paperback *Roots*.
Something that made how much?
Three hundred million dollars?
He was suing them for years.
The millions he made on TV *Roots* he spent a lot of it to
sue
Doubleday to get a better deal — I don't know if he ever
got it.
Roots was a devastation.
The tens of millions and hundreds of millions made on
Roots

went to produce,
not to make more Black series,
like *Roots,*
but they went to produce a *series*
maybe a dozen mini-series on *Jewish* history
as opposed to Black history.
You can document what was produced in terms of Black
history
compared to what was produced of Jewish history.
It's a devastation.
But the *one* thing that came out of this for me,
was that when these people told me, you know,
"We bought your research
We bought your history
You really have no ..."
I was thrown off
I had to get out of there.
I stayed for another couple of days.
I told Alex I had to make a pilgrimage to my grandfather's
grave.
Never knew my grandfather.
Then I watched one more scene in the Alex Haley thing
and that finished it for me.
A cutaway of a slave ship
that was so real that they had to bring in these high school
kids,
and once these high school kids played the enslaved
Africans greased
down in simulated vomit
and feces
they couldn't come back,
so they had to continue to get,
go take these youngsters,
and some little White woman
who was there sleeping with one of those guys,
they told her, "You cannot take these kids without
authorization."
But she would drive a bus

up to the schoolyard,
put the kids in it, and bring them to the set.
And it almost produced a riot
there.
But anyway this slave scene
was so realistic
the trainer's up on a lower deck
and Kunta Kinte's on a bottom deck
and they call down to each other,
and the trainer says,
"Kunta Kinte,
Be strong! Be strong!
We may have to fight.
Kill the White man and return to Mother Africa."
This was high drama.
All of us grown men over hiding in the shadows in *tears*.
Then
Green rushes out and said, "Break! Break!"
He said he didn't want the scene.
We said, "What?"
Even Lou Gossetts (sic) and them were ready to *fight!*
You know 'cause they had —
a movie script is just
a skeleton,
you have to put your soul in a movie script,
and they put their heart and soul into what would
    have been ...
And with the African —
because the "earth is mother" all over Africa.
So to say to go back to Mother Africa is a very
    meaningful phrase.
But this
Englishman refused
to accept it,
and they almost had a physical fight on the set.
They compromised and said,
"We – are – all – from – one – village,"
(Hitting his hand rhythmically on the desk.)

which is not the same thing.
After that I said, "I have to go."
I said I have to go,
and I rented a —
I flew out with Lorne Greene, of all people.
He saw me and we had known each other for a couple of
    weeks from
the set,
and he's sitting there drinking his little drinks
talking about "Isn't *Roots* wonderful.
It's everybody's history,"
and I'm dying.
(Pause.)
Get to Atlanta.
Rent a car. Cut across the Georgia countryside.
Came to a fork in the road,
made the right turn,
and there
on a bluff
was a clapboard church
made by my grandfather
and
four
other trustees.
Then when
I went across the cemetery
to see, uh,
the gravesite where he was —
the tallest tombstone in the graveyard was his.
Uhm,
it was an obelisk.
On it was a Masonic symbol.
He was the master of the lodge.
On it was his vital statistics:
"Born August the tenth 1868."
At the birth of the Fourteenth Amendment.
I later learned that his brother Sam was born
1865 at the birth of the Thirteenth Amendment!

And this is why people say,
"Who is he?
What is he?
Why is he?"
If they only know
I've had one of the best educations on the planet.
Yeah.
So ...
When I went to Albany
in July,
I went knowing that you might not have
much time,
just like my wife said on the radio today:
"When we speak
we speak as though it is the last speech we're gonna make."
But I knew what was at stake
ever since they branded me a conspiracy theorist,
February 12, 1990,
two-column editorial in the *New York Times*.
That was,
in the concept of Jewish thinking,
the kiss of death.
I knew I had been targeted.
Arthur Schlesinger went and wrote a book
called *The Disuniting of America*.
He has everybody in the margin
except a half-page photo of myself
which said to us,
"This is the one they got to kill."
We know that Schlesinger
and his people had sent out a thousand letters
to CEOs around the country
and foundation heads
not to have anything to do with
all of us involved in these studies
for multicultural curriculum
so, uh ...

Knowing that I had taken this beating for two and a
    half years
it was my chance to strike out,
but people don't understand
that that was my way of saying,
"You bastids! (sic) ...
for starting this process
for destroying *me*."
That was my striking out.
But people don't know the context.
They don't know that for two and a half years
I bore this burden
by myself
and I bore it well.
And now they've got a problem.
'Cause after they destroyed me,
here he is resurrected!!!!!
I spoke at Columbia, I spoke at Queens College....

LETTY COTTIN POGREBIN

Near Enough to Reach

Evening. The day before Thanksgiving, 1991. On the phone.
Direct, passionate, confident, lots of volume. She is in a
study with a rolltop desk and a lot of books.

I think it's about rank frustration and the old story
that you pick a scapegoat
that's much more, I mean Jews and Blacks,
that's manageable,
because we're near,
we're still near enough to each other to reach!
I mean, what can you do about the people who voted for
    David Duke?
Are Blacks going to go there and deal with that?
No, it's much easier to deal with Jews who are also panicky.
We're the only ones that pay any attention.
(Her voice makes an upward inflection. Listening on the phone.)
Well, Jeffries did speak about the Mafia being, um,
Mafia,
and the Jews in Hollywood.
I didn't see
this tremendous outpouring of Italian
reaction.
Only *Jews* listen,
only *Jews* take Blacks seriously,
only *Jews* view Blacks as full human beings that you
should *address*
in their rage
and, um,
people don't seem to notice that.

But Blacks, it's like a little child kicking up against Arnold
Shwartzenegger
when they,
when they have anything to say about the dominant culture
nobody listens! Nobody reacts!
To get a headline,
to get on the evening news,
you have to attack a Jew.
Otherwise you're ignored.
And it's a shame.
And we all play into it.

MINISTER CONRAD MOHAMMED

Seven Verses

April, 1992, morning. A café/restaurant. Roosevelt Island, New York. We are sitting in the back, in an area that is surrounded by glass floor-to-ceiling windows. Mr. Mohammed is impeccably dressed in a suit of an elegant fabric. He wears a blue shirt and a bow tie. He has on fine shoes, designer socks, and a large fancy watch and wedding ring. His hair is closely cropped. He drinks black coffee, and uses a few packs of sugar. He is traveling with another man, also a Muslim, in the clothing of a Muslim, impeccable, who sits at another table and watches us.

The condition of the Black man in America today is part
    and parcel,
through the devlishment
that permitted Caucasian people
to rob us of our humanity,
and put us in the throes of slavery ...
The fact that our — our Black
parents
were actually taken
as cattle
and as, as
animals
and packed into
slave ships
like sardines
amid feces
and urine —
and the suffering of our people,

for months,
in the middle passage —
Our women,
raped
Before our own eyes,
so that today
some look like you,
some look like me,
some look like brother ...
(Indicating his companion.)
This is a crime of tremendous proportion.
In fact,
no crime in the history of humanity
has before or since
equaled that crime.
The Holocaust did not equal it.
Oh, absolutely not.
First of all,
that was a horrible crime
and that is something that is a disgrace in the eyes of
    civilized
people.
That, uh, crime also stinks
in the nostrils of God.
But it in no way compares with the slavery of our people
because we lost over a hundred
and some say over two hundred and fifty,
million
in the middle passage
coming from Africa
to America.
We were so thoroughly robbed.
We didn't just loose six million.
We didn't just
endure this
for, for
five or six years
or from '38 to '45 or '39 to —

We endured this for over three hundred years —
the total subjugation of the Black man.
You can go into Bangladesh today,
Calcutta,
(He strikes the table with a sugar packet three or four times.)
New Delhi,
Nigeria,
some really
so-called underdeveloped nation,
and I don't care how low that person's humanity is
(He opens the sugar packet.)
whether they never
had running water,
if they'd never seen a television or anything.
They are in better condition than the Black man
    and woman
in America today
right now.
Even at Harvard.
They have a contextual understanding of what
    identity is.
*(He strikes the table with another sugar packet three or four times
    and opens it.)*
But the Black man has no knowledge of that;
he's an amnesia victim
(Starts stirring his coffee.)
He has lost knowledge of himself
(Stirring his coffee.)
and he's living a beast life.
(Stirring his coffee.)
So this proves that it was the greatest
crime.
Because we were cut off from our past.
Not only were we killed and murdered,
not only were our women raped
in front of their own children.
Not only did the master stick
(The spoon drops onto saucer.)

at times,
daggers into a pregnant woman's stomach,
slice the stomach open
push the baby out on the ground and crush the head
    of the baby
to instill fear in the Massas of the plantation.
(Stirring again.)
Not only were these things done,
not only were our thumbs
(Spoon drops.)
put in, in devices
that would just
slowly torture the slave
and tear the thumb off from the root.
Not only were we sold on the auction block
like cattle,
not permitted to marry.
See these are the crimes
of slavery that nobody wants to talk about.
But the most significant crime —
because we could have recovered from all of that —
but the fact that they cut off all knowledge from us,
told us that we were animals,
told us that we were subhuman,
took from us our names,
gave us names like
Smith
and Jones
and today we wear those names
with dignity
and pride,
yet these were the names given to us in one of the greatest
    crimes
ever committed on the face of the earth.
So this kind of thing,
Sister,
is what qualifies slavery
as the greatest

crime
ever committed.
They have stolen
our garment.
Stolen our identity.
The Honorable Louis Farrakhan
teaches us
that *we* are the chosen of God.
We are those people
that almighty God Allah
has selected as his chosen,
And they are masquerading in our garment —
the Jews.
We don't have an identity today.
Because we are the people ...
There are seven verses
in the Bible,
seven verses,
I believe it is in *Deutoronomy,*
that the Jews base
their chosen people, uh, uh,
claim the theology,
the whole theological exegesis
with respect
of being the chosen
is based upon seven verses
in the Scripture that talk
about a covenant
with Abraham.

LETTY COTTIN POGREBIN

Isaac

Morning. Spring. On the phone. She is in her office in her home on West 67th Street and Central Park West in Manhattan. Her office has an old-fashioned wooden rolltop desk and bookcases filled with books. She says she was wearing leggings and a loose shirt.

Well,
it's hard for me to do that
because
I think there's a tendency to make hay
with the Holocaust,
to push
all the buttons.
And I mean this story about my uncle Isaac — makes *me* cry
and it's going to make your audience cry
and I'm beginning to worry
that
we're trotting out our Holocaust stories
too regularly and that we're going to inure each other to
    the truth of
them.
But
I think
maybe if you let me read it,
I would prefer to read it:
(Reading from Debra, Golda and Me, Being Female and
    Jewish in America.*)*
"I remember my mother's cousin
Isaac who came to New York
immediately after the war and lived with us for several
    months.

Isaac is my connection to dozens of other family members who
were murdered in the concentration camps.
Because he was blond and blue-eyed he had been
chosen as the designated survivor of his town.
That is the Jewish councils had instructed him to do
    anything
to stay alive and tell the story.
For Isaac
anything turned out to mean this.
The Germans suspected his forged Aryan papers and
    decided that he
would have to prove by his actions that he was not a Jew.
They put him on a transport train with the Jews of his town
and then gave him the task of herding into the gas
    chambers
everyone in his train load.
After he had fulfilled that assignment
with patriotic
German efficiency,
the Nazis accepted the authenticity of his identity papers
and let him go.
Among those whom Isaac packed into the gas chambers
    that day
dispassionately as if shoving a few more items into an
    overstuffed
closet
were his wife
and
two children.
The designated survivor
arrived in America
at about age forty
(Breathes in.)
with prematurely white hair and a dead gaze within the
    sky blue
eyes that'd help save his life.
As promised he told his story to dozens of Jewish agencies

and community leaders and to groups of families and
     friends which
is how I heard the account
translated from his Yiddish
by my mother.
For months he talked,
speaking the unspeakable.
Describing a horror
that American Jews had suspected but could not conceive.
A monstrous tale
that dwarfed the demonology of legend
and gave me the nightmare I still dream to this day.
And as he talked
Isaac seemed to grow older and older
until one night
a few months later
when he finished telling everything he knew
he died."

ROBERT SHERMAN

Lousy Language

11:00 A.M. Wednesday, November 13, 1991. A very sunny and large, elegant living room in a large apartment near the Brooklyn Museum. Mr. Sherman is sitting in an armchair near an enormous bouquet of flowers for the birth of his first child. He wears sweats, and a bright orange long-sleeved tee shirt. Smiles frequently, upbeat, impassioned. Fingers his wedding ring. Each phrase builds on the next, pauses are all sustained intensity, never lets up. Full. Lots of volume, clear enunciation, teeth, and tongue very involved in his speech. Good-humored, seems to like the act of speech.

Do you have demographic information on Crown Heights?
The important thing to remember is that —
and again I will check these numbers when I get back to
    the office —
I think the
Hasidim
comprise only ten percent
of the population
of the neighborhood.
The Crown Heights conflict has been brewing on and off
    for twenty years
since the Hasidic community
developed some serious numbers
and some strength in Crown Heights and as African
    Americans and
Caribbean Americans came to make up the dominant
    culture in
Crown Heights.
Very important to remember that
those things that are expressed really as

bias,
those things
that we at the Human Rights Commission
would consider to be bias,
have the same trappings of bias,
which is complaints based on a characteristic, not on a
    knowledge of a
specific person.
There sort of is a soup
of bias —
prejudice, racism, and discrimination.
I think bias really does relate to
feelings with a valance,
feelings with a, uhm,
(Breathing in.)
feelings that can go in a direction positive or negative
although we usually use bias to mean a negative.
What it means usually
is negative attitudes
that can lead to negative behaviors:
biased
acts, biased incidents,
or biased crimes.
Racism is hatred based on race.
Discrimination refers to
acts against somebody ...
so that the words
actually tangle up.
I think in part
because vocabulary
follows general awareness....
I think you know
the Eskimos have seventy words for snow?
We probably have seventy different kinds of bias, prejudice,
    racism, and
discrimination,
but it's not in our mind-set to be clear about it,
so I think that we have

sort of lousy language
on the subject
and that
is a reflection
of our unwillingness
to deal with it honestly
and to sort it out.
I think we have very, very bad language.

CROWN HEIGHTS, BROOKLYN, AUGUST 1991

RABBI JOSEPH SPIELMAN

No Blood in His Feet

9:30 A.M. Tuesday, November 12, 1991. A large home on President Street in Crown Heights. Only natural light, not very much light. Dark wood. A darkish dining room with an enormous table, could seat twenty. The Rabbi sits at the head of the table. Lots of stuff on the table. He wears a black fedora, black jacket, and reading glasses. As he talks, he slightly slides around the tape-recorder microphone, which is in front of him at the table. The furniture in the dining room, including his chair, is, for the most part, very old, solid wood. There are children playing quietly in another room, and people come in and out frequently, but always whispering and walking carefully not to make noise, unless they speak to him directly. The children at one point come over and stare at me.

Many people were on the sidewalk,
talking, playing,
drinking
beer or whatever —
being that type of neighborhood.
A car
driven by an individual —
a Hasidic individual —
went through the intersection,
was hit by another car,
thereby causing it to go onto the sidewalk.
The driver on seeing
himself in such a position that he felt he was going to
     definitely hit
someone,
because of the amount of people on the sidewalk,

he steered at the building,
so as to get out of the way of the people.
Obviously, for the most part,
he was successful.
But regrettably,
one child was killed
and another child
was wounded.
Um,
seeing what happened,
he jumped out of the car
and, realizing
there may be a child under the car,
he tried to physically lift
the car
from the child.
Well, as he was doing this
the Afro-Americans were beating him already.
He was beaten so much he needed stitches in the scalp
    and the face,
fifteen or sixteen stitches
and also
there were three other passengers in the car
that were being beaten too.
One of the passengers was calling 911
on the cellular phone.
A Black person
pulled the phone out of his hand and ran.
Just stole the — stole the telephone.
The Jewish community
has a volunteer
ambulance core
which is funded totally from the nations —
there is not one penny of government funds —
and manned by volunteers —
who many times at their expense —
supplied the equipment that they carry in order to save
    lives.

As one of the EMS ambulances were coming,
one of the Hasidic ambulances or the Jewish ambulances
     came
on the scene.
The EMS responded with three ambulances on the scene.
They were there before
the Jewish ambulance came.
when the Jewish ambulance came,
two or three police cars were already on the scene.
The police saw the potential for violence
and saw that the occupants of the car
were being beaten and were afraid for their safety.
At the same time the EMS asked
the Hasidic ambulance for certain pieces of equipment
     that they
were out of,
that they needed to take care of the Cato kid,
and,
um,
in fact, I was ...
The Hasidic ambulance left, leaving behind one of the
     passengers.
That passenger had a walkie-talkie and he requested that I
come down to pick him up.
And at that time there was a lot of screaming and shouting
and it was a mixed crowd, Hasidic and Afro-American.
The police said, "Rabbi get your people out of here."
I told them to leave and I left.
Now,
a few hours later,
two and a half hours later,
in a different part of Crown Heights,
a scholar
from Australia,
Yankel Rosenbaum,
who, urr,
I think he had a doctorate or he was working on his
     doctorate,

was walking on the street
on his own —
I mean he was totally oblivious —
and he was accosted by a group of young Blacks
about twenty of them strong
which was being egged on by a Black
male approximately
forty years old and balding,
telling them,
"Kill all Jews —
look what they did to the kid
kill all Jews."
and all the epithets that go along with it,
"Heil Hitler" and all of it.
They stabbed him,
which later on the stab wounds were fatal
and he passed away in the hospital.
The Mayor,
hearing about the Cato kid,
came to the Kings County Hospital
to give condolences to the family of the child who had
    regrettably been killed.
At the meantime they had already wheeled in
Mr. Rosenbaum.
He was in the emergency room
and I was at the hospital at the same time,
and the Mayor, seeing me there,
expressed his concern
that a child,
uh, innocent child, had been killed.
Where I explained to him
the fact
that,
whereas the child was killed from an unfortunate accident
where there was no malicious intent,
here
there was an individual lying in the emergency room
who had been stabbed with malicious intent

and for the sole reason —
not that he did anything to anyone —
just from the fact that he happened to be Jewish.
And the Mayor went with me to the emergency room
to visit Mr. Rosenbaum.
This was approximately one and a half hours before he
     passed away.
I noticed at the time that his feet
were
completely white.
And I complained to the doctor
on the scene,
"He's having a problem with blood circulation
because there's no blood in his feet."
And she gave me some asinine answer.
And the Mayor asked her what his condition is:
"Serious but stable."
In the meantime he was screaming and in pain
and they weren't doing anything.
Subsequently they, um,
they started giving him anaesthesia in a time that
they weren't allowed to give him anesthesia
and while he was under anesthesia,
he passed away.
So there was totally mismanagement in his case.
So whereas the Mayor,
had been fed ...
his people got
whatever information he got out of the Black community
     was
that
the driver had run a red light
and also,
and that the ambulance,
the Hasidic ambulance,
refused to take care of the Black child that was dying and
rather took care of their own.
Nenh?

And this is what was fed amongst the Black community.
And it was false,
it was totally false
and it was done maliciously
only with the intent to get the riots,
to start up the resulting riots.

THE REVEREND CANON
DOCTOR HERON SAM

Mexican Standoff

*November 12, 1991. 4:00 P.M. The rectory office at St.
Mark's Church in Crown Heights. A small, short office.
Lived in but impeccably ordered. Some light from lamps,
some from overhead. Plaques and awards everywhere. The
reverend is wearing a yellow shirt, priest's collar, tan summer jacket. He wears spectacles. There are clocks that make
noise and sound the hour in his office and outside the
church bells sound during the interview, loud. Throughout
the talk he is trying to get the corner of a calendar to stay
down, but it continues to stick up. Finally he uses a paper-
weight to keep it down.*

You can't have that kind of accident
if people are observing the speed limits.
People knew it was the Grand Rebbe.
People have seen the Grand Rebbe
charging through the community.
He is worried
about a threat on his life
from the Satmars.
These Lubavitcher people
are really very,
uh, enigmatic people.
They move so easily between
simplicity and sophistication.
Because
they fear for his life,
because the Satmars
who are their sworn enemies
(He laughs, chuckles.)

have threatened to *kill*
the Rebbe.
So whenever he comes out
he's gotta be *whisked!*
You know like a President
or even better than a President.
He says he's an intuhnational figuh (sic)
like a Pope!
I say
then, "Why don't you get Swiss guards
to escort you
rather than using the police
and taxpayers' money?"
He's gotta be
whisked!
Quickly through the neighborhood.
Can't walk around.
He used to walk.
When I first came here.
Now he doesn't walk at all.
They drive him.
And when he walked
you could tell he was in front
because there was,
he was protected all around
and they spilled out onto the streets
and buses had to stop
Because this BIG BAND
had to escort
the Rebbe from his house over there
to the synagogue.
So the Rebbe goes to the cemetery.
Every time the Rebbe goes to the cemetery,
which is once a week
to visit his wife — dead wife —
and father-in-law,
the police
lead him in escort

charging down the street
at seventy miles an hour in a metropolis —
what do you want?
(Swift increase in volume and suddenly businesslike.)
It happened that on this occasion that as they were coming
    back,
uh,
the police car
with its siren,
had gone over a main
intersection with the light
in favor
of the police car.
The Rebbe's Cadillac had passed
when the lights had become amber
and nobody expected the bodyguard van,
uh,
station wagon
to deliberately go through the red light.
So the traffic
that had the right of way kept coming and
BANG!
came the collision and the careening
onto the sidewalk
had to damage whoever was there
and then, um, they were more concerned about licking their
    own
wounds.
Rather than to pick
the car off the boy
who died as a result.
And then the ambulance that came —
turned out to be a Hasidic ambulance
the Jewish ambulance —
was concerned about the people in the van
while some boy lay dead,
a Black boy lay dead on the street.
The people showed their anger,

(Increase in volume.)
they burned and whatever else,
upturned
police cars
and looted,
and as a result,
I think in retaliation, murdered one of the Hasidics.
But that was just the match that lit the powder keg.
It's gonna happen again and again.
It's a Mexican standoff right now.
But it's gonna happen again.

ANONYMOUS YOUNG MAN #1

Wa Wa Wa

7:00 or 8:00 P.M. Spring. A recreation room at Ebbets Field apartments. A very handsome Caribbean American man with dreadlocks, in his late teens or early twenties, wearing a bright, loose-fitting shirt. The room is ill equipped. There are a few pieces of broken furniture. It is poorly lit. A woman, Kym, with dreadlocks and shells in her hair, is at the interview. It was originally scheduled to be her interview. The Anonymous Young Man #1 and the other Anonymous Young Man, #2, started by watching the interview from the side of the room but soon approached me and began to join in. Anonymous Young Man #1 was the most vocal. Anonymous Young Man #2 stood lurking in the shadows. A third young man, younger than both of them, wearing wire spectacles and a blue Windbreaker, who looks quite like a young Spike Lee, sat silent with his hands and head on the table the entire time. There is a very bad radio or tape recorder playing music in the background.

What I saw was
she was pushin'
her brother on the bike like
this,
right?
She was pushin'
him
and he kept dippin' around
like he didn't know how
to ride the bike.
So she kept runnin'
and pushin' him to the side.

So she was already runnin'
when the car was comin'.
So I don't know if she was runnin' towards him
because we was watchin' the car
weavin',
and we was goin'
"Oh, yo
it's a Jew man.
He broke the stop light, they never get arrested."
At first we was laughin', man, we was like
you see they do anything
and get away with it,
and then
we saw that he was out of control,
and den
we started regrettin' laughin',
because then
we saw where he was goin'.
First he hit a car, right,
he tore the whole front fender off a car,
and then we was like
Oh
my God,
man, look at the kids,
you know,
so I was already runnin' over there
by the time the accident happened.
That's how we know he was drinkin'
'cause he was like
Wa Wa Wa Wa
and I was like
"Yo man he's drunk.
Grab him,
grab him.
Don't let him go anywhere"
I said,
"Grab him."

I didn't want him to limp off
in some apartment somewhere
and came back in a different black jacket.
So I was like,
"Grab him,"
and then I was like, "Is the ambulance comin' for the kids?"
'Cause I been in a lot of confrontations with Jews before
and I know that when they said an ambulance
is comin'
it most likely meant for them.
And they was like,
"oh, oh."
Jews right?
"Ambulance comin', ambulance comin',
calm down, calm down,
God will help them,
God will help them if you believe."
And he was actin' like he was dyin'.
"Wa Aww,
me too,
I'm hurt, I'm hurt, I'm hurt too."
Wan nothin' wrong with him
wan nothin' wrong with him.
They say that we beat up on that man
that he had to have stiches because of us.
You don't come out of an accident like that unmarked,
without a scratch.
The most he got from us was slapped
by a little kid.
And here come the ambulance
and I was like, "That's not a city ambulance,"
not like this I was upset right
and I was like,
"YO,
the man is drunk!
He ran a red light!
Y'all ain't gonna do nothin'."

Everybody started comin' around, right,
'cause I was talkin' about
these kids is dyin' man!
I'm talkin' about the skull of the baby is on the ground
    man!
and he's walkin'!
I was like, "Don't let him get into that ambulance!"
And the Jews,
the Jews
was like private, private ambulance
I was like, "Grab him,"
but my buddies was like,
"We can't touch them."
Nobody wanted to grab him,
nobody wanted to touch him,
An' I was breakin' fool, man,
I was goin' mad,
I couldn't believe it.
Everybody just stood
there,
and that made me cry.
I was cryin'
so I left, I went home and watched the rest of it on TV,
it was too lackadazee
so it was like me, man, instigatin' the whole thing.
I got arrested for it
long after
in Queens.
Can't tell you no more about that,
you know.
Hey, wait a minute,
they got eyes and ears everywhere.
What color is the Israeli flag?
And what color are the police cars?
The man was *drunk,*
I open up his car door,
I was like, when —

I was like, "He's been drinkin'!"
I know our words don't have no meanin',
as Black people in Crown Heights.
You realize, man,
ain't no justice,
ain't never been no justice,
ain't never gonna be no justice.

MICHEAL S. MILLER

"Heil Hitler"

*A large airy office in Manhatten on Lexington in the fifties.
Mr. Miller sits behind a big desk in a high-backed swivel
chair drinking coffee. He's wearing a yarmulke. Plays with
the swizzel stick throughout. There is an intercom in the office, so that when the receptionist calls him, you can hear it,
and when she calls others in other offices, you can hear it,
like a page in a public place, faintly.*

I was at Gavin Cato's funeral,
at nearly every public event
that was conducted by the Lubavitcher community and
    the Jewish
community as a whole
words of comfort
were offered to the family of Gavin Cato.
I can show you a letter that we sent
to the Cato family expressing, uh,
our sorrow over the loss,
unnecessary loss, of their son.
I am not aware of a word
that was spoken at that funeral.
I am not aware of a —
and I was taking notes —
of a word that was uttered
of comfort to the family of Yankele Rosenbaum.
Frankly this was a political rally rather than a funeral.
The individuals you mentioned —
and again,
I am not going to participate in verbal acrimony,
not only
were there cries of, "Kill the Jews"

or,
"Kill the Jew,"
there were cries of, "Heil Hitler."
There were cries of, "Hitler didn't finish the job."
There were cries of,
"Throw them back into the ovens again."
To hear in *Crown Heights* —
and Hitler was no lover of Blacks —
"Heil Hitler"?
"Hitler didn't finish the job"?
"We should heat up the ovens"?
From *Blacks?*
Is more inexplicable
or unexplainable
or any other word that I cannot fathom.
The hatred is so
deep seated
and the hatred
knows no boundaries.
There is no boundary
to anti-Judaism.
The anti-*Judaism* —
if people don't want me
to use,
hear me use the word anti-Semitism.
And I'll be damned if,
if preferential treatment is gonna
be the excuse
for a single bottle
rock,
or pellet that's, uh, directed
towards a Jew
or the window of a Jewish home
or a Jewish store.
And, frankly,
I think the response of the Lubavitcher community was
    relatively
passive.

HENRY RICE

Knew How to Use Certain Words

Thursday, November 21, 1991. The Jackson Hole restaurant on Lexington in the thirties in Manhattan. Lunchtime, dimly lit, a reddish haze on everything, perhaps from a neon light. Mr. Rice, very neatly dressed, is eating a large, messy hamburger and horizontally chopped pickles. Drinking a Miller Lite. Beer is in a bottle next to a red plastic glass. He's wearing a baseball cap over very closely cut hair and a very bright, multicolored, expensive-looking colored nylon jacket. Heavy new Timberland boots. Struggling to eat without making a mess of the food. At some point sits up from food and has his right hand or fist on his hip – a very unaffected but truly authoritative stance. Good-natured, handsome, healthy. A song like Patsy Cline's "Crazy"* is very loud on the jukebox. [I urge you to try and obtain the rights to use this song.]

I went back home and got my bike
because I knew I would have to be
illusive.
I was there in body and in spirit
but I didn't participate in any of the violence
because basically I have a lot to lose.
But I was there
and I would have defended myself if it was necessary,
most definitely.
I weaved around trouble.
When something broke out, I moved back,
when it calmed down, I would move back in on the
    front line.

---

* See Special Note on Songs and Recordings on copyright page.

I was always there.
And Richard Green heard me saying something to a bunch
   of kids
about *voting*
about the power of *vote*
the power of *numbers*
And he said,
uh,
I said, "Get away from me, you're an Uncle Tom,
get away from me.
Get back in your Mercedes-Benz!"
No! I said that to Clarence Norman
and to Richard Green,
both of them.
I was tearing them apart.
Richard Green was very persistent.
He said,
"Look Mr. Rice,
I like the way you speak
I need you.
Please help me.
I'm a community activist....
ba, ba, ba, ba, ba."
(He drops some food on his clothes, or so it seems, he looks and
   grins.)
It didn't get on me.
"I'm a community activist.
I need your help,
please help me,"
and so forth.
Again,
I didn't pay him no mind
but we spoke
some
the next day after that,
after the incidents that took place on that corner
of Albany Avenue.
A brother was beat up —

cops rushing into the Black crowd
didn't rush into the Jewish crowd,
cops rushed into the Black crowd
started beatin' up
Black people.
But the next day Richard came by in a yellow van,
a New York City Department of Transportation van,
with a megaphone,
yellow light flashing,
(Music segues from a song like Patsy Cline's "Crazy" to one such
as Public Enemy's "Can't Truss It,"* or Naughty by Nature's
"O.O.P."*)*
the whole works
and, um,
he said,
"Henry, I need you in this van.
Drive around with me.
Let's keep some of these kids off the street tonight."
I said, "Okay."
He said,
"The blood
of Black men is on your hands tonight!"
I said, "Okay."
We drive around in the van,
"Young people stay in the house!
Mothers keep your children in the house,
please."
So I began fillin' (sic)
I began feeling like
I had to do it
after he told me that,
"the blood of the Black man"
were on my hands,
you know,
Richard Green sure know how to use certain words.

* See Special Note on Songs and Recordings on copyright page.

(He giggles.)
I remember reaching Albany Avenue —
kids were being chased by the police.
I jump out with a portable megaphone,
I tell them, "Stop running!
The cops won't chase you!
and they won't hit you!"
The next thing I know,
cop grabs my megaphone, hits me in the head with a stick,
handcuffs me,
and takes the megaphone out of my hand.
So I'm like,
"Wait a minute
I'm doing a community service for the Mayor's office."
They don't want to hear it.
Matter of fact,
they still have the megaphone 'til this day.
I'm like,
"Richard Green get me
out of this police car, please!"
So a Black captain came by,
thank God,
and he says, "What's goin' on?"
Richard Green explained it to him.
He said, "Let him go."
Get back in the van,
there's another Brother in the van,
starts saying,
"Non violence!"
to the young Brothers.
They begin throwing bottles at the, uh,
at the van.
One guy got so upset
he had a nine-millimeter
fully loaded.
He said, "Get the hell out of this neighborhood!"
I told Richard Green, "Take me on home. Shit!"
The next day

more violence:
fires,
cars being burnt,
stores being broken into,
a perception that Black youth
are going crazy in Crown Heights
like we were angry over
nothing,
understand?

NORMAN ROSENBAUM

My Brother's Blood

A Sunday afternoon. Spring. Crisp, clear, and windy. Across from City Hall in New York City. Crowds of people, predominately Lubavitcher, with placards. A rally that was organized by Lubavitcher women. All of the speakers were men, but the women stand close to the stage. Mr. Rosenbaum, an Australian, with a beard, hat, and wearing a pinstriped suit, speaks passionately and loudly from the microphone on a stage with a podium. Behind him is a man in an Australian bush hat with a very large Australian flag which blows dramatically in the wind. It is so windy that Mr. Rosenbaum has to hold his hat to keep it on his head.

Al do lay achee so achee aylay alo dalmo
My brother's blood cries out from the ground.
Let me make it clear
why I'm here.
In August of 1991,
as you all have heard before today,
my brother was killed in the streets of Crown Heights
for no other reason
than that he was a Jew!
The only miracle was
that my brother was the only victim
who paid for being a Jew with his life.
When my brother was surrounded,
each and every American was surrounded.
When my brother was stabbed four times,
each and every American was stabbed four times
and as my brother bled to death in this city,

while the medicos stood by
and let him bleed
to death, it was the gravest of indictments against this
    country.
One person out of the twenty gutless individuals
who attacked my brother has been arrested.
I for one am not convinced that it is beyond the ability of
    the New York police
to arrest others.
Let me tell you, Mayor Dinkins,
let me tell you, Commissioner Brown:
I'm here,
I'm not going home,
until there is justice.

NORMAN ROSENBAUM

16 Hours Difference

7:00 A.M., Spring. Newark Airport, Departure Gate, Continental Airlines. Mr. Rosenbaum is moments before his flight to Los Angeles and then back to Australia. Wearing a pinstriped suit. Hat. Suitcase. He has sparkling blue eyes with a twinkle, rosy cheeks, and a large smile throughout the interview.

There's sixteen hours difference between New York and
    Melbourne
and I had just gotten back to my office
and I had a phone call from my wife,
and she said she wanted me to come home straight away
and I sensed the urgency in her voice.
I said, "are you all right?" She said, "Yeah."
I said, "are the children all right, you know the kids?" She
    says, "yeah."
So I'm driving home and I'm thinking, I wonder what's the
    problem now, you know?
We had some carpenters doing some work, I wonder if
    there has been a disaster,
some sort of domestic problem,
and I thought, oh my God, you know, my parents,
I didn't even ask after them,
how insensitive not to even ask after my parents,
And I've got a grandmother eighty-five years old, same sort
    of thing.
So I get home,
I walk in the door,
and a friend of mine was standing there,

close friend,
does the same sort of work as me, he's a barrister and an
    academic,
and he sees me and he says,
"There's got a pro —
uh,
we've got a problem.
There's a problem."
I thought he was talking about a case we were working on
    together,
he says, " 'Z come,
come and sit down."
He goes to me,
"There's been a riot in New York,
been a riot in Crown Heights,
Yankel's been stabbed and he's dead."
And
my brother was the last in the world,
I hadn't even given him a thought.
I mean the fact that my brother
could be attacked
or die,
it just hadn't even entered my mind.
At first I appeared all cool, calm and collected.
I then
started asking questions
like who told you,
how do you know,
are you sure?
I just asked the question,
you know,
are you sure?

ANONYMOUS YOUNG MAN #2

Bad Boy

Evening. Spring. The same recreation room as interview with Anonymous Young Man #1. Young Man #2 is wearing a black jacket over his clothes. He has a gold tooth. He has some dreadlocks, and a very odd-shaped multicolored hat. He is soft-spoken, and has a direct gaze. He seems to be very patient with his explanation.

That youth,
that sixteen-year-old
didn't murder that Jew.
(Pause.)
For one thing,
he played baseball, right?
He was a atha-lete,
right?
A bad boy
does
bad things.
Only a bad boy coulda stabbed the man.
Somebody who
does those type a things,
or who sees
those type a things.
A atha-lete
sees people,
is interested in athletics,
stretchin',
excercisin',
goin' to his football games,
or his baseball games.

He's not interested
in stabbin'
people.
So
it's not in his mind
to stab,
to just jump into somethin',
that he has no idea about
and
sta —
and kill a man.
A bad boy,
somebody who's groomed in badness,
or did badness
before,
stabbed the man.
Because I used to be a atha-lete
and I used to be a bad boy,
and when I was a atha-lete,
I was a atha-lete.
All I thought about was atha-lete.
I'm not gonna jeoparsize (sic) my athleticism
or my career to do anything
that bad people do.
And when I became a bad boy
I'm not a atha-lete no more.
I'm a bad boy,
and I'm groomin' myself in things that is bad.
You understand, so
he's a atha-lete,
he's not a bad boy.
It's a big difference.
Like,
mostly the Black youth in Crown Heights have two things
    to do —
either DJ or be a bad boy, right?
You either

DJ, be a MC, a rapper
or Jamaican rapper,
ragamuffin,
or you be a bad boy,
you sell drugs and rob people.
What do you do?
I sell drugs.
What do you do?
I rap.
That's how it is in Crown Heights.
I been livin' in Crown Heights mosta my life.
I know for a fact that that youth, that sixteen-year-old,
didn't kill that Jew.
That's between me and my Creator.

SONNY CARSON

Chords

Lunchtime. Spring. A fancy restaurant in Brooklyn. Sonny tells me it's where all the judges come for lunch. White linen tablecloths. Light wood walls, lamplight next to the table. Tile floor. He is eating crab cakes. He is dressed in a black turtleneck and a gray jacket. He has on a mud cloth hat. He has an authority stick with him, and lays it on the table. His bodyguard, wearing a black leather jacket, enters in the middle of the interview. Sonny chides him for being late.

It's going to be a long hot summer.
I'm connected up with the young people all over the
    country
and there's a thread
leading to an eruption
and Crown Heights began the whole thing.
And the Jews come second to the police
when it comes to feelings of dislike among Black folks.
The police,
the police,
believe me, the police —
I know the police and the police know me
and they turned that whole place into an occupied camp
with the Seventy-first Precinct as the overseers.
And don't think that everything is OK within that precinct
    among those officers
either.
Don't think that,
don't think that.
You know the media has always painted me as the bad
    guy —
that's OK!
I'm a good guy to pick on.

Their viewers don't like me either,
they really don't like me because I *am* the bad guy,
I am the ultimate bad guy
because of my relationship to the young people in the city.
I understand their language.
I respect them as the future.
I speak their language. They don't even engage in long
    dialogue
anymore
just short.
"Word."
It always amazes me
how the city fathers,
the power brokers,
just continue to deny what's happening.
And it is just getting intolerable for me to continue to
    watch
this small
arrogant
group of people continue to get this kind of preferential
    treatment.
They sit on the school board.
A board of nine,
and they have
four members, and their kids don't even go to public
    school!
So that's the kind of arrogance I'm talking about.
I have no reason to be eagerly awaiting the coming together
    of our
people.
They owe me first.
I'm not givin' in just like that,
I don't want it.
You can have it.
Like my grandmother said,
"Help the bear."
If you see me and the bear in a fight,

help the bear —
don't help me,
help the bear.
I don't need any of it from them!
And I'm not gonna advocate any coming together and
  healing of
America
and all that shit.
You kiddin'?
You kiddin'?
Just 'cause I can have the fortune of walking in here
and sitting and talking
and having a drink,
it appears that I have all the same kinds of abilities
of other folks in here.
No, it's not that way.
'Cause tonight
by nighttime it could all change for me.
So I'm always aware of that, and that's what keeps me goin'
today
and each day!
(He eats.)
I have
this idea
about a film.
See,
these kids, they got
another kinda rhythm now,
there's a whole new kinda
step that they do.
When I first heard rap
I was sittin' in a huge open kinda stadium,
boys and girls high school field,
and I heard these kids come out and start rappin',
and I'm listening
but it's not really clickin',
but I was mesmerized though.
But it was simontaneous (*sic*)

all around the country
and I said, "Oh shit,"
and everybody I knew who was young was listenin' to it
and I said, "Wow."
Because I have always been involved with young people
and all of a sudden I got it,
I really heard the rhythm,
the chords,
the discord.
There's a whole new sound
that the crackers are tryin' to get, but they can't get it.
I heard it on a television commercial.
One of the most beautiful pieces of art
that I ever witnessed
was a play
called
um,
um,
um,
'bout, 'bout the Puerto Rican gang —
no, no, no, no, no —
the Puerto Rican gang,
the musical
that was on Broad —
yeah,
West Side Story —
the answer should be
a musical.

RABBI SHEA HECHT

Ovens

Morning. Spring. A building on Eastern Parkway. A large
room with a very long conference table. There are pictures of
Lubavicher men on the walls. Rabbi Hecht is wearing a
shirt, open at the neck. He has several crisp one-dollar bills
in his shirt pocket. These are, apparently, dollar bills that the
Rebbe has given him. It is a custom that the Rebbe gives out
one-dollar bills on Sunday. Rabbi Hecht has a beard. He
wears glasses, traditional Hasidic garb, including tsitses
(ceremonial fringes that hang over his belt), and a red
yarmulke with gold trim which is ripped. His daughter comes
in frequently to get money from him. He keeps telling her to
wait until he is finished. She becomes more and more agi-
tated. His brother also enters frequently to ask him questions,
and to tell him he's late.

What is my goal?
My goal is not
to give anybody a message
that we plan on working things out
by integrating
our two
things.
By a person understanding more of their own religion
they will automatically respect another person.
The respect that my religion teaches me has nothing to do
with understanding you.
See, there's a problem.
If
the only way I'm going to respect you
is based on how much I understand you,

no matter what it is
in certain circles you're gonna run into problems.
Number one,
we are different,
and we think we should and can be different.
When the Rebbe said to the Mayor
that we were all
one people,
I think
what the Rebbe is talking about is that,
that common denominator that we're all children of God,
    and the
respect we all have to give each other under that banner.
But that does not mean that I have to invite you to my
    house for
dinner,
because I cannot go back to your home for dinner,
because you're not gonna give me kosher food.
And I said,
so, like one Black said,
I'll bring in kosher food.
I said eh-eh
We can't use your ovens,
we can't use your dishes,
it's, it —
it's not just a question of buying certain food,
it's buying the food,
preparing it a certain way.
We can't use your dishes, we can't use your ovens.
The — the higher you go
the more common denominator.
And what the Rebbe was saying,
you as the Mayor
don't get caught up in the differences,
you're —
from your position is —
you have to look at it as one city
and one

human race.
We are all New Yorkers!
And therefore I will protect all New Yorkers.
You see
preferential treatment
suggests
that you're giving the person
the police car
not because they need the police car
but because
they are who they are.
You're not gonna
give them the housing
because they
need the housing —
you're giving it because of who they are.
But
just because I'm a Jew
therefore I
shouldn't get the police car?
The question is
a synagogue
that has five thousand Jews
leave
the synagogue
at the same time,
do they have a police car to stop the traffic?
The answer is every — single — synagogue,
temple,
mosque,
in
the
world
stops traffic
when five thousand people have to walk out
at the same time.

THE REVEREND AL SHARPTON

Rain

As before.

The D.A.
came back with no indictment.
Uh, so then our only course
was to ask for a special prosecutor
which is appointed by the Governor,
who's been hostile,
and to sue civilly.
When we went into civil court
we went to get an order to show cause.
The judge signed it and gave me a deadline of three days.
The driver left the country....
No one even said, "Why would he run?
If he did no wrong?"
If you and I were in an accident we'd have to go to civil
    court.
Why is this man
above the law?
So they said, "He's in Israel."
So I said,
"Well, I'll go to Israel to show best effits."
And the deadline
was,
I had to serve him by Tuesday,
which was Yom Kippur —
that was the judge's decision not mine.
So we went.
Alton Maddox and I

got on a plane,
left Monday night,
landed Tuesday morning,
went to the American embassy, uh,
so that
if this man had any decency at all
he could come to the American Embassy and receive service,
which he has not done to this day.
Came back,
went to court
and showed the judge the receipts,
and the judge said, "You made best effits,"
therefore you are now permitted,
by default,
to go ahead
and sue the rabbi or whomever
because you cannot do the driver."
So it wasn't just a media grandstand.
We wanted to show the world
one, this man *ran*
and was *allowed* to run, and, two we wanted to be able to
    legally go
around him,
to sue the people he was working for so that we can bring
    them into
court and establish *why* and what happened.
And it came out in the paper the other day
that the driver in the other car didn't even have a
    driver's license.
So we're dealing with a *complete* outrage here,
we're dealing with a double standard,
we're dealing with uh, uh, a, a
situation where
Blacks do not have equal protection under the law
and the media is used to castigate us
that merely asked for justice
rather than castigate those that would hit a kid
and walk away like he just stepped on a roach!

Uh,
there also is the media
contention of the young Jewish scholar
that was stabbed that night
and they've even distorted
saying *my words at the funeral.*
I *preached* the funeral.
Uh, [the newspaper said I]
helped to, to, uh, uh,
spark or, or, or, or, or *inspire* or *incite* people to kill him
    [Yankel Rosenbaum]
when he was dead the day before
I came out there.
He was killed the night
that the young man
was killed with the car accident.
I didn't even get a call
from the family
'til eighteen hours later.
So there's a whole media distortion
to protect them [the Lubavitchers].
Nobody is talking about,
"Why
is this guy
in flight?"
If I was a rabbi
(I am a ministuh)
and my driver hit a kid,
I would not let the driver *leave*
and I certainlih would give my condolences,
or anything else I could,
to the family,
I don't care what race they are.
To this minute the Rebbe has never even uttered a word of
sympathy
to the family,
not even sent 'em a *card*
a *flower* or *nothing!*

And he's supposed to be a religious leader.
So it's treating us with absolute contempt
and I don't care how controversial it makes us.
I *won't* tolerate being insulted.
If you piss in my face I'm gonna call it *piss*.
I'm not gonna call it rain.

RICHARD GREEN

Rage

2:00 P.M. in a big red van. Green is in the front. He has a driver. I am in the back. Green wears a large knit hat with reggae colors over long dreadlocks. Driving from Crown Heights to Brooklyn College. He turns sideways to face me in the back, and bends down, talking with his elbow on his knee.

Sharpton, Carson, and Reverend Herbert Daughtry
didn't have any power out there really.
The media gave them power.
But they weren't turning those youfs on and off.
Nobody knew who controlled the switch out there.
These young people had rage like an oil-well fire
that have to burn out.
All they were doin' was sort of orchestratin' it.
Uh, they were not really the ones that were saying, "Well
stop, go, don't go, stop, turn around, go up."
It wasn't like that.
Those young people have rage out there,
that didn't matter who was in control of that —
that rage had to get out
and that rage
has been building up.
When all those guys have come and gone,
that rage is still out here.
I can show you that rage every day
right up and down this avenue.
We see, sometimes in one month, we see three bodies
in one month. That's rage,
and that's something that nobody has control of.
And I don't know who told you that it was preferential

treatment for

Blacks that the Mayor kept the cops back....

If the Mayor had turned those cops on?

We would still be in a middle of a battle.

And

I pray on both sides of the fence,

and I tell the people in the Jewish community the
same thing,

"This is not something that force will hold."

Those youfs were running on cops without nothing
in their hands,

seven- and eight- and nine- and ten-year-old boys were
running at

those cops

with nothing,

just running at 'em.

That's rage.

Those young people out there are angry

and that anger has to be vented,

it has to be negotiated.

And they're not angry at the Lubavitcher community

they're just as angry at you and me,

if it comes to that.

They have no

role models,

no guidance

so they're just out there growin' up on their own,

their peers are their role models,

their peers is who teach them how to move

so when they see the Lubavitchers

they don't know the difference between "Heil Hitler"

and, uh, and uh, whatever else.

They don't know the difference.

When you ask 'em to say who Hitler was they wouldn't even
be able

to tell you.

Half of them don't even know.

Three quarters of them don't even know.

(Phone rings, Richard picks it up, it's a mobile phone.)
"Richard Green, can I help?
Aw, man I tol' you I want some color
up on that wall. Give me some colors.
Look, I'm in the middle of somethin'."
(He returns to the conversation.)
Half them don't even know three quarters of 'em.
Just as much as they don't know who Frederick Douglass
was.
They know Malcolm
because Malcolm has been played up to such an event now
that they know Malcolm.
But ask who Nat Turner was or Mary MacCloud Bethune or
Booker T.
Because the system has given 'em
Malcolm is convenient and
Spike is goin' to give 'em Malcolm even more.
It's convenient.

ROSLYN MALAMUD

The Coup

Spring. Midafternoon. The sunny kitchen of a huge, beautiful house on Eastern Parkway in Crown Heights. It's a large, very well-equipped kitchen. We are sitting at a table in the breakfast nook area, which is separated by shelves from the cooking area. There is a window to the side. There are newspapers on the chair at the far side of the table. Mrs. Malamud offers me food at the beginning of the interview. We are drinking coffee. She is wearing a sweatshirt with a large sequined cat. Her tennis shoes have matching sequined cats. She has on a black skirt and is wearing a wig. Her nails are manicured. She has beautiful eyes that sparkle, are very warm, and a very resonant voice. There is a lot of humor in her face.

Do you know what happened in August here?
You see when you read the newspapers.
I mean my son filmed what was going on,
but when you read the newspapers....
(Responding to a question.) Of course I was here!
I couldn't leave my house.
I only would go out early during the day.
The police were barricading here.
You see,
I wish
I could just like
go on television.
I wanna scream to the whole world.
They said
that the Blacks were rioting against the Jews in Crown
    Heights
and that the Jews were fighting back.

Do you know that the Blacks who came here to riot were
    not my
neighbors?
I don't love my neighbors.
I don't know my Black neighbors.
There's one lady on President Street —
Claire —
I adore her.
She's my girlfriend's next-door neighbor.
I've had a manicure
done in her house and we sit and kibbitz
and stuff
but I don't know them.
I told you we don't mingle socially
because of the difference
of food
and religion
and what have you here.
But
the people in this community
want exactly
what I want out of life.
They want to live
in nice homes.
They all go to work.
They couldn't possibly
have houses here
if they didn't
generally — They have
two,
um,
incomes
that come in.
They want to send their kids to college.
They wanna live a nice quiet life.
They wanna shop for their groceries and cook their meals
    and go to
their Sunday picnics!

They just want to have decent homes and decent lives!
The people who came to riot here
were brought here
by this famous
Reverend Al Sharpton,
which I'd like to know who ordained him?
He brought in a bunch of kids
who didn't have jobs in
the summertime.
I wish you could see the *New York Times*,
unfortunately it was on page twenty,
I mean, they interviewed
one of the Black girls on Utica Avenue.
She said,
"The guys will make your pregnant
at night
and in the morning not know who you are."
(Almost whispering.)
And if you're sitting on a front stoop and it's very, very hot
and you have no money
and you have nothing to do with your time
and someone says, "Come on, you wanna riot?"
You know how kids are.
The fault lies with the police department.
The police department did nothing to stop them.
I was sitting here in the front of the house
when bottles were being thrown
and the sergeant tells five hundred policemen
with clubs and helmets and guns
to duck.
And I said to him,
"You're telling them to duck?
What should I do?
I don't have a club or a gun."
Had they put it —
stopped it on the first night
this kid who came from Australia ...

(She sucks her teeth.)
You know,
his parents were Holocaust survivors, he didn't have to die.
He worked,
did a lot of research in Holocaust studies.
He didn't have to die.
What happened on Utica Avenue
was an accident.
JEWISH PEOPLE
DO NOT DRIVE VANS INTO SEVEN-YEAR-OLD BOYS.
YOU WANT TO KNOW SOMETHING? BLACK PEOPLE DO
    NOT DRIVE
VANS INTO SEVEN-YEAR-OLD BOYS.
HISPANIC PEOPLE DON'T DRIVE VANS INTO SEVEN-
    YEAR-OLD BOYS.
IT'S JUST NOT DONE.
PEOPLE LIKE JEFFREY DAHMER MAYBE THEY DO IT.
BUT AVERAGE CITIZENS DO NOT GO OUT AND TRY
    TO KILL
(Sounds like a laugh but it's just a sound.)
SEVEN-YEAR-OLD BOYS.
It was an accident!
But it was allowed to fester and to steam and all that.
When you come here do you see anything that's going on,
    riots?
No.
But Al Sharpton and the likes of him like *Dowerty*,
who by the way has been in prison
and all of a sudden he became Reverend *Dowerty* —
they once did an exposé on him —
but
these guys live off of this,
you understand?
People are not gonna give them money,
contribute to their causes
unless they're out there rabble-rousing.
My Black neighbors?

I mean I spoke to them.
They were hiding in their houses just like I was.
We were scared.
I was scared!
I was really frightened.
I had five hundred policemen standing in front of my house
every day
I had mounted police,
but I couldn't leave my block,
because when it got dark I couldn't come back in.
I couldn't meet anyone for dinner.
Thank God, I told you my children were all out of town.
My son was in Russia.
The coup
was exactly the same day as the riot
and I was very upset about it.
He was in Russia running a summer camp
and I was very concerned when I had heard about that.
I hadn't heard from him
that night the riot started.
When I did hear from him I told him to stay in Russia,
    he'd be safer
there than here.
And he was.

REUVEN OSTROV

Pogroms

9:00 P.M. November 1991. In a basement of a Crown Heights house. Mr. Ostrov wears a yarmulke. Eating popcorn and sliced apples. Very low, gentle-sounding nigunim *music plays in the background, it almost sounds like New Age music, perhaps because traditional music is played on a modern electronic keyboard instrument. In the show, I wore a basketball jacket with project CURE's insignia, which Mr. Ostrov did not do at this interview, but previously had at a basketball game. He is clean-shaven, which is unusual for a Lubavitcher man his age. He had chosen to shave his beard. He has a very rich, deep voice.*

I was working in a hospital.
I work as an assistant chaplain at
Down State Kings County Hospital.
I heard that Yankel Rosenbaum was stabbed and, um, they
were gonna give an *aurtopsy*
and they asked if he had an
aurtopsy
or not because in the Jewish religion a person is not
    allowed to have
an aurtopsy
and I found out later that he did have one
a few days later.
I found a Jewish man in a room,
a Russian man.
His mother committed suicide
because she was, uhm, she was terrified.
She jumped out of the third floor of her apartment
    building,

committed suicide.
The mother originally came from Russia.
I was speaking to her son
in one of the rooms near the morgue
trying to get his mother not to have an aurtopsy
and he was telling me that the mother
came from Russia eleven years ago
and the mother left Russian eleven years ago
because of the hardships that they had over there,
and when they came to America
and when this thing started to happen in Crown Heights.
It became painful
and it felt like, like there was no place to go.
It's like you're trapped,
everywhere you go there's Jew haters.
And then he told me she commit suicide,
told me the next morning he woke up
he heard the doorbell ring.
He wasn't,
she wasn't there.
He noticed that the window was open,
which is never open
because she was afraid of the cold
even in the summertime.
And he saw his mother
with blood all over her
landed head first
on the concrete side of the apartment building.
After that we already knew this was getting serious,
because we had,
we had Sonny Carson come down
and we had, um,
Reverend Al Sharpton come down
start making pogroms.

CARMEL CATO

Lingering

7:00 P.M. The corner where the accident occurred in Crown Heights. An altar to Gavin is against the wall where the car crashed. Many pieces of cloth are draped. Some writing in color is on the wall. Candle wax is everywhere. There is a rope around the area. Cato is wearing a trench coat, pulled around him. He stands very close to me. Dark outside. Reggae music is in the background. Lights come from stores on each corner. Busy intersection. Sounds from outside. Traffic. Stores open. People in and out of shops. Sounds from inside apartments, televisions, voices, cooking, etc. He speaks in a pronounced West Indian accent.

In the meanwhile
it was two.
Angela was on the ground
but she was trying to move. Gavin was still.
They was trying to pound him.
I was the father.
I was 'it, chucked, and pushed,
and a lot of
sarcastic words were passed towards me
from the police
while I was trying to explain: It was my kid!
These are my children.
The child was hit you know.
I saw everything, everything,
the guy radiator burst
all the hoses,
the steam,
all the garbage buckets goin' along the building.
And it was very loud,

everything burst.
It's like an atomic bomb.
That's why all these people
comin' round
wanna know what's happening.
Oh it was very outrageous.
Numerous numbers.
All the time the police sayin'
you can't get in,
you can't pass,
and the children laying on the ground.
He was hit at exactly eight-thirty.
Why?
I was standing over there.
There was a little child —
a friend of mine
came up with a little child —
and I lift the child up
and she look at her watch at the same time
and she say it was eight-thirty.
I gave the child back to her.
And then it happen.
Um, um ...
My child, these are the things I never dream about.
I take care of my children.
You know it's a funny thing,
if a child get sick and he dies
it won't hurt me so bad,
or if a child run out into the street and get hit down,
it wouldn't hurt me.
That's what's hurtin' me.
The whole week
that Gavin died
my body was changing,
I was having different feelings.
I stop eating,
I didn't et
nothin',

only drink water,
for two weeks;
and I was very touchy —
any least thing that drop
or any song I hear
it would effect me.
Every time I try to do something
I would have to stop.
I was
lingering, lingering, lingering, lingering,
all the time.
But I can do things,
I can see things,
I know that for a fact,
I was telling myself,
"Something is wrong somewhere,"
but I didn't want to see,
I didn't want to accept,
and it was inside of me,
and even when I go home I tell my friends,
"Something coming I could feel it
but I didn't want to see."
And all the time I just deny deny deny,
and I never thought it was Gavin,
but I didn't have a clue.
I thought it was one of the other children —
the bigger boys
or the girl,
because she worry me,
she won't et —
but Gavin 'ee was 'ealtee,
and he don't cause no trouble.
That's what's devastating me now.
Sometime it make me feel like it's no justice,
like, uh,
the Jewish people,
they are very high up,
it's a very big thing,

they runnin' the whole show
from the judge right down.
And something I don't understand:
The Jewish people, they told me
there are certain people I cannot be seen with
and certain things I cannot say
and certain people I cannot talk to.
They made that very clear to me — the Jewish people —
they can throw the case out
unless
I go to them with pity.
I don't know what they talkin' about.
So I don't know what kind of crap is that.
And make me say things I don't wanna say
and make me do things I don't wanna do.
I am a special person.
I was born different.
I'm a man born by my foot.
I born by my foot.
Anytime a baby comin' by the foot
they either cut the mother
or the baby dies.
But I was born with my foot.
I'm one of the special.
There's no way they can overpower me.
No there's nothing to hide,
you can repeat every word I say.

PROPERTY PLOT

NTOZAKE SHANGE:
    Cigarette (lit)
ANONYMOUS LUBAVITCHER WOMAN:
    Clothes for folding
GEORGE WOLFE:
    Tray with:
        tea pot with tea
        cups
        creamer with cream
RIVKAH SIEGAL:
    Coffee mug
MINISTER CONRAD MOHAMMED:
    Coffee cup with coffee
    Spoon
    Packets of sugar
LETTY COTTIN POGREBIN:
    Book
RABBI JOSEPH SPIELMAN:
    Reading glasses
    Tape recorder and microphone
REVEREND CANON DOCTOR HERON SAM:
    Spectacles
    Calendar
    Paperweight
MICHAEL S. MILLER:
    Coffee cup with coffee
    Swizzel stick
HENRY RICE:
    Large hamburger
    Chopped pickles
    Miller Lite beer
    Red plastic glass
NORMAN ROSENBAUM:
    Suitcase

SONNY CARSON:

    Crab cakes

    Authority stick

RABBI SHEA HECHT:

    Crisp one-dollar bills (several)

ROSYLN MALAMUD:

    Coffee cups with coffee

    Food

REUVEN OSTROV:

    Popcorn

    Sliced apples

    Basketball